SIMPLE
PRINTMAKING

SIMPLE
PRINTMAKING
Peter Weiss

illustrations by Sally Gralla

Lothrop, Lee & Shepard Company
A Division of WILLIAM MORROW & COMPANY, INC.
New York

COPY 6

1 2 3 4 5 80 79 78 77 76

Library of Congress Cataloging in Publication Data

Weiss, Peter (date)
  Simple printmaking.

  SUMMARY: A beginner's guide to printmaking, including tips on creating prints from found objects or materials from nature, printing with rollers and stencils, marbling, and printing on fabric.
  1. Prints—Technique. [1. Prints—Technique. 2. Handicraft]
I. Gralla, Sally. II. Title.
NE860.W423   760'.2'8   75-31762
ISBN 0-688-41735-3
ISBN 0-688-51735-8 lib. bdg.

Also by Peter Weiss

Balsa Wood Craft

Cutting Up With Paper: A Craft Book
(by Peter and Carol Weiss)
illustrated by Sally Gralla

Contents

SIMPLE PRINTMAKING

Tools
and
Materials

This book explores various quick, easy, and inexpensive print-making techniques. Most of the prints on the following pages were made using only ink, paper, a small paintbrush, and a few ordinary household tools and materials.

Work Space

The first thing you need is a place to work—a desk or a table with enough room for your brushes and ink and a good supply of paper. Printmaking can be pretty messy, so protect your desk or table top with several layers of old newspapers. Have a rag or some paper towels handy, for wiping up spills and cleaning ink from your hands.

Ink

Always use water soluble printing ink. Water soluble ink dries quickly and can be cleaned up easily with soap and warm water. It is much easier to work with than the old-fashioned oily type of ink. The oily kind of ink takes a long time to dry,

11

and special solvents are needed to wash it from your hands, brushes, and tools. Water soluble ink will wash off glass, metal, and ceramic materials without leaving any stains.

Paper

It is a good idea to have two or three different kinds of paper on hand. Any one print will look slightly different on each type of paper that you use. Get a supply of newsprint, or some cheap paper, for making sample prints and experimenting with new printmaking ideas. Try printing on construction paper, typing paper, or a pad of inexpensive letter-writing paper. Try making the same print on two kinds of paper that are very different from each other—a thin, smooth-surfaced paper and a thick, soft, absorbent paper. Look for paper in

the school and office supply departments of a five-and-ten or a discount department store.

For making stencil prints, you may want to buy a small package of stencil paper (see p.68).

When you have made a print that looks really good on ordinary paper, try printing it again on a sheet of colored tissue paper, textured rice paper, or some other fancy type of paper from an art supply store.

Brushes

You will need two or three cheap paintbrushes, in various sizes. Use a brush size that seems appropriate for each different type of printmaking project—a small brush for inking small objects, and a bigger brush for inking printing blocks or other large objects. The largest brush used in making the prints for this book was a flat paintbrush measuring ¾ inch across the bristles.

Try to find brushes in a five-and-ten or a discount store. Art supply stores sell many different kinds of brushes, but the prices there are usually higher. You might want to buy a stippling brush (see p.68), if you plan to make a lot of stencil prints.

You will also need a jar or a can of water, for rinsing out brushes and thinning your ink. Do not let ink dry on your brushes. Leave dirty brushes in the jar of water until you get a chance to wash them with soap and water.

Cutting Tools

Scissors will be needed for many of the printmaking projects in this book.

For a few projects, you will need to use a cutting tool with a very sharp blade—an x-acto knife or a single-edge razor blade. Use only single-edge blades. Do not use a regular double-edge razor blade. They are not safe to hold in your hands. An x-acto knife is even safer and easier to use than a single-edge razor blade. An x-acto knife is a small metal handle with removable blades.

Single-edge razor blades are sold in drugstores, super-markets, and discount department stores. X-acto knives are sold in hobby shops and art supply stores. If you enjoy work-ing on handicraft projects, it is worth spending a little extra money to buy an x-acto knife.

Glue

Several types of printmaking call for the use of glue. The best glue for most purposes is an ordinary white household glue, such as Elmer's Glue-all. This kind of glue dries quickly, con-tains no dangerous chemicals, and comes in a reclosable plastic squeeze bottle that is very easy to use. For a few projects, you may need a bottle or can of rubber cement. White glue and rubber cement can be found wherever school and office supplies are sold.

Cardboard

Some printmaking methods involve gluing various materials to pieces of cardboard. Use the thickest, strongest cardboard that you can find. Thin cardboard can be used, but it may curl and twist out of shape from contact with wet glue or ink. Thick, heavy cardboard holds its shape better. Ask at a grocery store for an empty cardboard carton. Cut pieces of cardboard from the carton, using a sharp kitchen knife, a single-edge razor blade, or an x-acto knife.

If you plan to make many prints from one cardboard print-ing block, try using the cardboard back from a used-up pad of paper, or buy a sheet of stiff, hard illustration board at an art supply store.

Stamp Pad

When you are making a print by stamping small objects on paper, pressing the objects on a well-inked stamp pad will be much faster and easier than inking them with a brush. Squeeze out some ink on the stamp pad. Work the ink into the pad with a damp brush. Add a drop of water from time to time, to prevent the ink from drying out. When you are not using it, close the stamp pad and wrap it in a plastic bag. This will keep the ink from hardening on the pad.

Use a new stamp pad for each different color ink that you use.

Stamp pads can be bought in the office supply department of a five-and-ten or a discount store.

Brayers

A brayer is a rubber roller that can be used to spread a thin, even coat of ink, or to press a sheet of paper smoothly and evenly on an inked surface. Brayers are expensive. Even a small one may cost two or three dollars. A large brayer, with a sturdy handle and a soft rubber roller, may cost ten dollars or more. Make a number of large prints without using a brayer, then decide whether or not you want to buy one.

Using a brayer can make a noticeable difference in the way a print turns out, especially with certain types of large block prints, since a brayer spreads the ink very smoothly, and leaves no dark or blotchy spots.

Brayers come in many different sizes. Buy a very small one, to begin with. If you decide to buy another, larger brayer, you can use the small one for spreading ink on a printing block, and use the larger one for pressing paper firmly against the inked block.

Brayers can be purchased in art and photography supply stores.

15

Other Materials

Various materials, such as string, felt, styrofoam, or clay, may be needed for certain printmaking projects. Before you begin working on a new type of print, read the instructions and make sure that you have all the materials needed.

Printmaking Tips

Start with the simplest printmaking projects, like leaf prints (p. 45), or styrofoam drawings (p. 83).

Squeeze out only a small amount of ink at a time. Leftover ink will harden and be wasted.

Your ink will last longer, and your prints will dry faster if you thin the ink slightly with water. Squeeze out a small amount of ink on a dish, a flat metal pan, or a double thickness of waxed paper. Thin the ink by stirring it with a damp brush.

If your ink is too thick, your prints will look dark and blotched. If your ink is too thin and watery, your prints may look faded or sloppy.

Always make two or three copies of each print. Study the first one and try to correct any flaws. Try using more or less ink, or try changing the way you press the inked surface on the paper.

Wipe up any spilled ink as soon as you notice it. Cleaning up is much easier when the ink is still wet.

Try combining two different printmaking methods on one sheet of paper. You could make a potato print (p. 31) on a marbled background (p. 77), or you could make your own greeting cards with stencil printed designs (p. 68). *Let the first print dry before making another print on the same piece of paper.*

Prints from Found Objects

Look for small objects with interesting shapes or textures. Each object must have a flat surface that can be pressed on a sheet of paper.

ABOVE: *Coins make interesting prints.*

BELOW: *Print made from washers, screw heads, and assorted machine parts.*

Look in a toolbox for washers, nuts, and nails or screws with flat heads. Look at the bottoms of things: salt shakers, wooden spools, old flashlight batteries, spice jars, etc. Look at the tops of things: plastic bottle caps, cork ends, lids from candy or cookie tins, caps from used-up toothpaste tubes, etc.

Thoroughly ink a small stamp pad. Make sample prints of the objects you have found. Press each object on the stamp pad and then on a sheet of paper. If you do not have a stamp pad, use a small paintbrush to spread ink on the objects to be printed.

You can create attractive designs just by printing the same object several times.

A die (above) and bottle bottoms (below) make attractive designs when printed several times.

Prints using bottle bottoms (above) and washers (below).

For more variety, try printing with colored ink, or with white ink on black paper. Use a different stamp pad for each color ink. If you are inking the objects with a brush, wash the brush before changing colors.

This design was made by using the base of a Magic Marker to print with white ink on black paper.

Try using two objects to print a simple repeating pattern.

Here a Magic Marker base and a machine part were used in a simple repeating pattern.

Combine a few different prints to build up a picture or an abstract design.

A plastic bottle cap, a die, a Magic Marker base, a machine part, and pieces of wooden matchsticks were used to create the following designs.

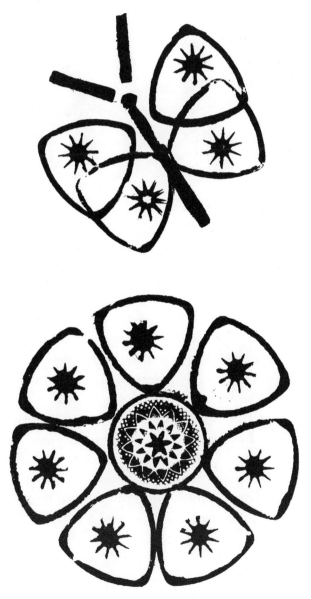

Only small objects can be inked by pressing them on a stamp pad. Larger objects should be inked with a brush.

A brayer (see p. 15) is useful for making prints from large objects. Brush ink on an object, cover it with a sheet of paper, and roll over the paper with the brayer. If you do not have a brayer, ink the object, cover it with paper, and rub the paper lightly with your fingers. Be careful not to shift the paper from side to side when you rub it.

Make two or three prints of each object. The first print is usually not the best. Each print will be different, depending on how much ink you use, how wet the ink is, and how hard you press on the paper when you make the print.

Wash each object (unless you are going to throw it away) as soon as you have made the last print.

ABOVE: *Print of the top of a candy tin.*

BELOW: *Print of the top of a stamped metal jewel box.*

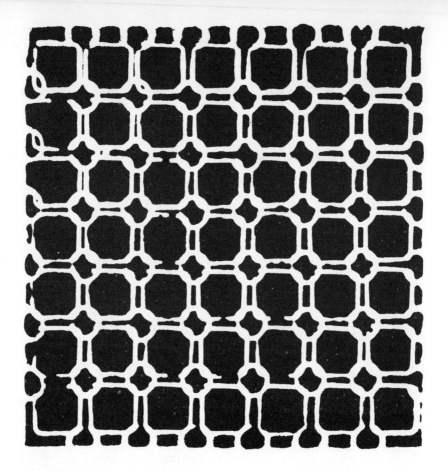

These designs are from the top and sides of a wooden box.

This print was made using the styrofoam tray from a package of chopped meat.

Soft, flexible objects should be inked with a brush and pressed between two clean sheets of paper. Roll over the top sheet of paper with a brayer, or rub it with your fingers, or press down on it with a piece of thick cardboard.

Print of a paper doily

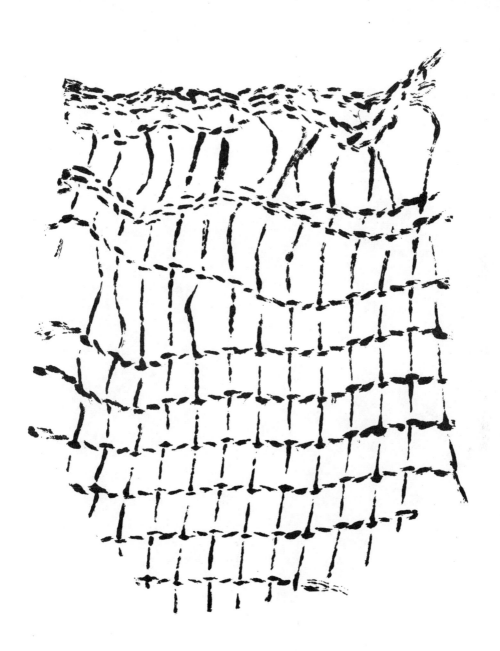

A section of a mesh potato sack

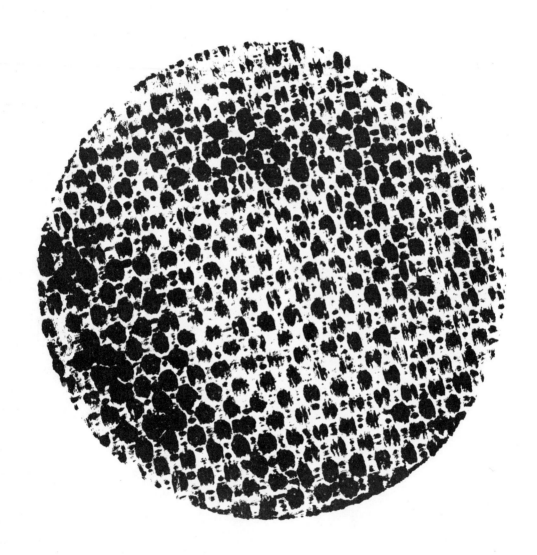

A woven straw hotplate

Carved Printing Stamps

Potato Prints

Cut a potato in half. Using a pencil point, lightly scratch the outline of a flower, or some other simple shape, on one half of the cut potato.

Using a small, sharp kitchen knife, make a shallow cut along the outline of your design. Carefully hollow out the part of the potato inside the outline. Do not cut all the way through the potato. Just scoop out enough of the potato so that your design is completely sunk into the flat surface.

Brush the potato with ink. The juice of the potato will mix with the ink, so you will not need to thin the ink with water. Press the inked potato firmly on a sheet of paper.

Carve another potato printing stamp, but this time cut away the part of the potato outside your scratched outline.

Make a design by combining prints from two or three different carved potato stamps.

For a print with a larger or more complicated pattern, use the largest potato you can find.

Eraser Stamps

Buy a few soft rubber erasers. Draw on each eraser the outline of the shape you want to print. Copy some of the shapes shown here, or make up your own.

If you want to print your own greeting card designs, draw simple holiday shapes on the erasers—a star, a candy cane, an Easter egg with a zig-zag stripe across it, a valentine heart, a pilgrim hat, etc.

Use an x-acto knife or a single-edge razor to cut away the rubber outside the outlines you have drawn. For printing stamps with hollow centers or textured patterns, cut holes or grooves in the eraser. Ink the erasers by pressing them on a stamp pad, or apply the ink with a small brush.

These designs were made with various combinations of the printed shapes shown above.

Clay Stamps

Buy a small package of water soluble clay, the kind used for making pottery (available at hobby shops and art supply stores).

Protect your table top with plenty of old newspapers. Spread a sheet of waxed paper on top of the newspapers. Fill a small bowl with water. Have a rag ready, so that you can wipe your hands when you are done working with the clay.

Unwrap the package of clay. Wet your hands in the bowl of water. Form some of the clay into a flattened hamburger shape, or any other flat shape that you like. Cover the clay with a sheet of waxed paper. Press the clay firmly with a smooth, hard object, like a book or the bottom of a frying pan. Peel off the top sheet of waxed paper. Use a sharp kitchen knife to carve a design into the surface of the clay, but *not* all the way through it.

Make smaller printing stamps with the leftover clay, or store it in a tightly closed glass jar.

Let your printing stamp dry for at least four or five days. Sandpaper any rough spots on the surface of the carved design. Bake the printing stamp in an oven for about two hours, using medium heat. This will harden the clay and make it less breakable. Wait for the clay to cool. Ink the design and press it on paper.

This clay stamp design was printed with white ink on black construction paper.

The following illustrations are patterns from clay printing stamps made in Mexico hundreds of years ago. These stamps were used to print colored designs on fabric and leather. If you want to print your own designs on fabric, see p.113.

From Enciso: DESIGN MOTIFS OF ANCIENT MEXICO, *Dover Publications, Inc.*

ABOVE: *From Enciso:* DESIGN MOTIFS OF ANCIENT MEXICO, *Dover Publications, Inc.*

OPPOSITE: *Animal designs from African art. From Williams:* AFRICAN DESIGNS, *Dover Publications, Inc.*

Nature
Prints

Weathered Wood

Find some pieces of wood that have been outdoors for a long time. Exposure to the weather brings out the grain of the wood. Wind, rain, and snow gradually wear away the softer parts of the wood, leaving a pattern of raised ridges.

If you live in a city, look for weathered wood in a vacant lot or near a construction site. If you live in the country, look for broken pieces of siding from an old shed or barn.

Brush ink on a piece of wood. Cover the wood with a sheet of paper. Roll over the paper with a brayer, or rub the paper with your fingers.

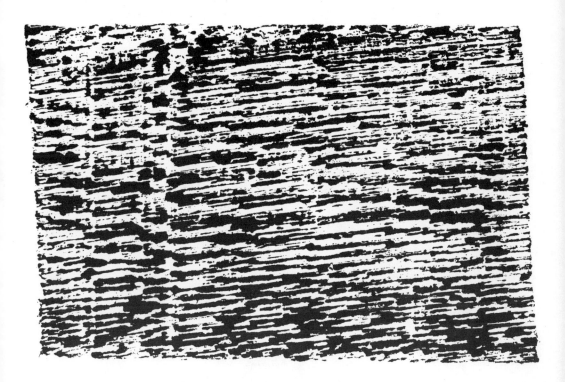

Leaf Prints
Gather some leaves from various shrubs and trees. Press the leaves between the pages of a book. Leave them in the book for a few days, until they will lie completely flat on a sheet of paper.

Leaves that are smooth and glossy will print as solid dark shapes. For prints with more variety of texture, look for leaves with veins running through them, or leaves with fuzzy or pebbled surfaces.

Brush a leaf with ink. Place it between two clean sheets of paper. Roll over the top sheet of paper with a brayer, or press down on the paper with a piece of stiff cardboard.

This printmaking method will also work with feathers, small weeds, bunches of wild grass, branches from ferns, and small clusters of pine needles.

Try printing leaves or feathers with white ink on dark paper, or with brightly colored ink on soft pastel colored paper. Use green ink and a cluster of pine needles to print your own Christmas cards.

Cross Sections

Look for fruits and vegetables that can be sliced in half to make printing stamps with interesting shapes.

ABOVE: *Apple, cut across core*
RIGHT: *Avocado with pit removed*
BELOW: *Apple, cut along core*

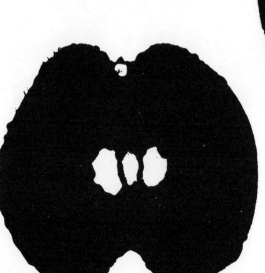

This method works best with fruits and vegetables with hollow spots in their centers. Ones with pulpy centers are more difficult to print, since the pulp tends to smear the ink.

Cross section of a tangerine

Repeated design using cross section of a peanut shell

Look for other natural forms that can be cut or broken in half and printed in cross section. Try using peanut, walnut, or almond shells, green peppers, ham or steak bones, or anything else you can think of.

Use a sharp knife to trim away any parts of a fruit or vegetable that have been in contact with printing ink. Wash the fruit or vegetable very thoroughly before eating it, to remove all traces of ink.

Fish Prints

Anyone who enjoys going fishing should try this quick and easy printing technique.

Dry a freshly caught fish with a rag or a paper towel. Brush one side of the fish with ink. Press the fish on a sheet of paper. A fish with a fairly flat body will give the best results. If the fish has a rounded body, you may need to roll it slightly from side to side to make sure that the whole shape gets printed.

Special precautions must be taken to make sure that the fish will be safe to eat. Make only one or two prints of each fish. Use only water soluble ink. Work as quickly as possible. As soon as you have finished printing, wash the fish very thoroughly. Scrub it with a brush, if necessary, to remove every trace of printing ink. Scale and clean the fish as usual. Do not eat the fish if the ink has gone through the skin and stained the flesh.

Mexican roller printing patterns from Enciso: DESIGN MOTIFS OF
ANCIENT MEXICO, *Dover Publications, Inc.*

Roller Printing

Found Objects

Look around your house or apartment for rounded objects with textured sides. Look for empty bottles and jars with patterns molded into the glass. Look for round candy or cookie tins with designs stamped into the metal sides. Check for things that are going to be thrown away: empty food containers, wheels from broken toys, used-up lipstick tubes—anything that will roll. Brush ink on the objects and roll them on paper.

Roller printed designs make nice borders for posters, signs, and home-made greeting cards. This method is also good for printing your own gift-wrap paper. Experiment with colored inks and large sheets of colored tissue paper (available at art supply stores).

It is not always necessary to ink the whole object. Ink only the part with the pattern that you want to print. The two prints following were made by inking the decorative rims around the bottoms of instant coffee jars.

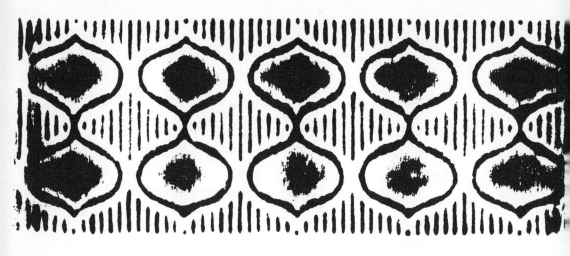

Roller prints of a bicycle tire (opposite) and a corn cob (below).

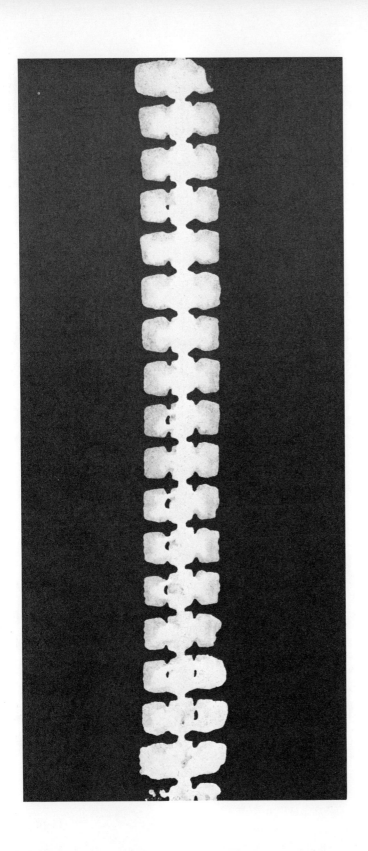

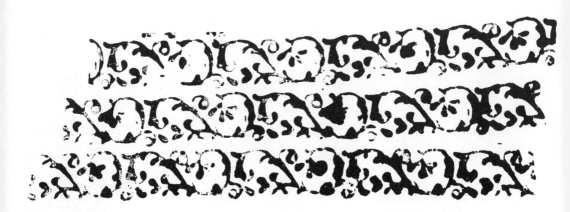

OPPOSITE PAGE: *Roller prints using a plastic bottle cap, the cap from a lipstick tube, and a lipstick tube.*

BELOW: *An unusual glass jar was used to create this design.*

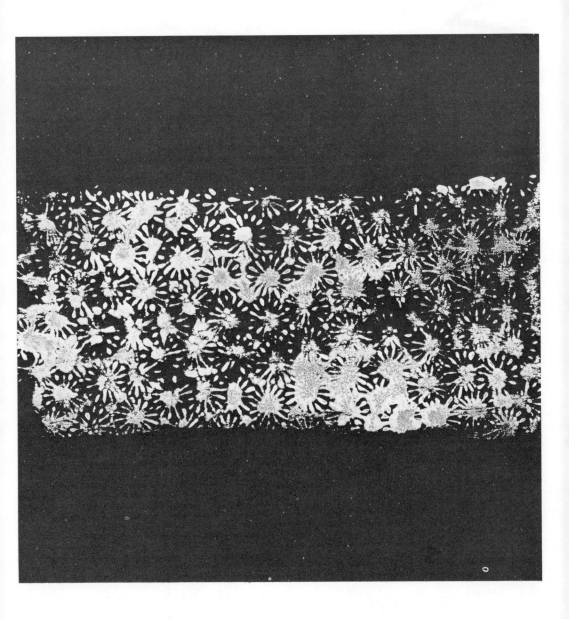

String Rollers

Wrap some string, thread, or yarn around a small glass jar. Glue the loose ends to the glass. Ink the jar and roll it on a sheet of paper. Rolling the jar in two directions will result in

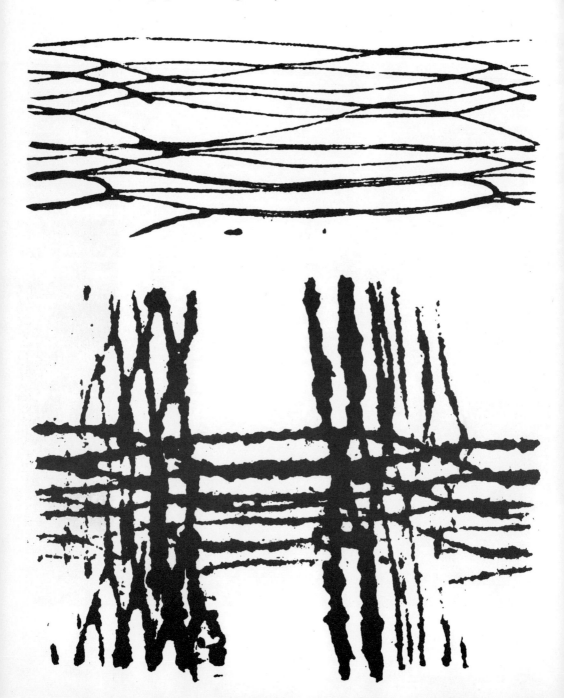

a print with a plaid pattern. Each material that you use will roll a different kind of printed line. Try slipping a few rubber bands around a jar.

Soda Bottle Rollers

Find a large soda bottle with a tight styrofoam wrapper. Several brands of soda pop come in bottles with this kind of wrapper. Use a ball-point pen to draw a design on the styrofoam. Press hard enough to leave a groove in the styrofoam. Ink the bottle and roll it on paper.

Cork Rollers

Collect some corks from empty wine bottles, or buy some corks at a hardware store. Use an x-acto knife or a single-edge razor blade to cut holes and slits in the sides of a cork. Do not try to cut away large chunks of cork at one stroke. Carefully cut out just a small bit of cork at a time.

Push a small nail into each end of the cork. You will be able to hold the nails and roll the cork like a rolling pin. Ink the cork and roll it on paper.

A tapered cork will roll in a curved line across the paper. A cork with straight sides (with both ends the same size) will roll in a straight line.

As soon as the cork has rolled one full turn the print will start looking faded and thinly inked. If you want to print a continuous strip, ink the cork again and start where the last roll ended.

Felt Cutout Rollers

Cut some small decorative shapes from scraps of felt. (You can buy felt scraps at most large fabric stores.) Try cutting flower and leaf shapes, or bird or animal shapes, or small geometric shapes—circles, squares, and triangles. Glue your felt cutouts to the cardboard tube from a roll of toilet paper. Let the glue dry for several hours.

Thin some printing ink with water. Brush ink on the felt cut-outs. Wait a few minutes for the ink to soak into the felt, then ink the cutouts again. Roll the tube on paper.

Felt will absorb quite a lot of ink, so your felt roller will make a long strip of printed designs before it needs to be inked again. Try using this method to make printed borders on posters or signs.

Stencil Printing

Before you buy any special stencil printing equipment, try making some prints using a regular small paintbrush and stencils cut from ordinary paper. If you enjoy this method of printmaking, buy a package of stencil paper and a small stippling brush. Both are available in art supply stores.

Stencil paper is a stiff, waxy paper that will not get soft or soggy from contact with wet ink. Using stencil paper, you will be able to make prints with sharper edges and a neater overall appearance.

A stippling brush has all its bristles cut to the same length. The shortest brush in the picture on p. 12 is a stippling brush. A stippling brush is used to dab on ink with an up and down motion, so that only the tips of the bristles touch the paper. This up and down motion of the brush prevents the ink from being pushed sideways under the edges of your stencils. You can save money by using a soft-bristled old toothbrush instead of a stippling brush, but the shape and weight of a stippling brush make it easier to work with.

Folded Cutout Stencils

Fold a square piece of paper in half. Fold it in half again, the other way. Use scissors to cut notches or small curved shapes from the folded edges of the paper. Unfold the paper and flatten it out. You will have a stencil with cut out areas in a symmetrical snowflake pattern.

Place the stencil on top of a blank sheet of paper. Hold the stencil down to keep it from moving while you make your print. Ink your brush lightly. Dab ink through the cutout holes in the stencil, using an up and down motion of the brush.

Try using a Magic Marker to make a stencil print. Sometimes this method can be easier than using ink.

Try cutting a row of linked paper dolls from a folded strip of paper. Unfold the strip of paper and make a stencil print of the cutout paper doll shapes.

Flat Cutout Stencils

Protect your table top with a piece of heavy cardboard or a thick pad of old newspapers. Place a sheet of paper on top of the cardboard or newspapers. Pin down the corners with thumbtacks. Use an x-acto knife or a single-edge razor blade to cut a design of small slits or holes in the paper.

Place the finished stencil on top of a blank sheet of paper. If your stencil design is large or very complex, you may want to pin down the stencil with thumbtacks. Dab ink carefully through the holes in the stencil.

Try building up a larger design by printing the same small cutout stencil several times. *Let the ink on each print dry completely before you make another print next to it.*

Print your initials in thick block letters on a sheet of paper. Make sure that the letters touch each other, so that you will be able to cut out the stencil in one piece. Cut around the outline of the letters. Cut out any enclosed spaces inside the letters. Make a silhouette print of your initials by dabbing around the letters with a lightly inked brush. The examples shown were done with a stippling brush.

These are traditional cut paper designs from China. Try making a flat cutout stencil using a simplified version of one of these designs. The white areas would be the holes in the stencil.

From Hawley: CHINESE FOLK DESIGNS, *Dover Publications, Inc.*

Cheesecloth and Paper Stencils

Buy a small scrap of cheesecloth, or some other light, open-weave fabric. All you need is a piece slightly larger than the paper that you plan to print on.

Staple strips of cardboard along the edges of the cheese-cloth. If you have no stapler available, glue each edge of the cheesecloth between two strips of cardboard. These card-board strips will hold the cheesecloth flat and keep it from moving when you brush on the ink.

Make a design from scraps of paper. Spread glue near the edges of each paper scrap. Press the cheesecloth onto the paper scraps.

When the glue is dry, turn the cheesecloth over on top of a sheet of paper. Dab ink on the cheesecloth with a stippling

brush, if you have one. If you use a lot of ink, you will get a print with a solid background. If you use less ink, the background will show the texture of the cheesecloth.

Marbling

Buy a small bottle of paint thinner and one or two bottles of model airplane enamel (available at toy stores and hobby shops). The marble prints shown here were all made with either black or white enamel, but you can use any colors you like.

Fill a shallow pan with about ¼ inch of water. Use a tooth-pick to scatter a few drops of enamel on the water. The enamel will float on top of the water. Stir the water with the toothpick until you get a pattern that you want to print. Drop a piece of paper gently on to the surface of the water. Remove the paper and set it aside to dry. Scatter a few more drops of enamel and make another marble print. Each print will be different, depending on how you stir the water. Try using two colors at once, but do not stir too hard, or the colors will just run together.

Marbled paper will wrinkle as it dries. It can be flattened out again by pressing it between two sheets of paper with a warm iron. Any kind of paper can be used for marbling, but

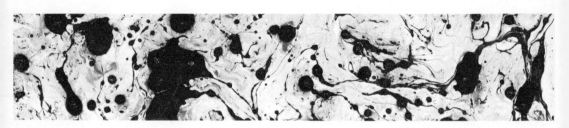

there will be less wrinkling if you use a coated paper such as
shelf paper (available in a five-and-ten or a discount store).

When you finish printing, or when you want to change
colors, soak up the excess enamel by spreading a paper napkin
on the water. Clean your hands and the pan with paint thinner.

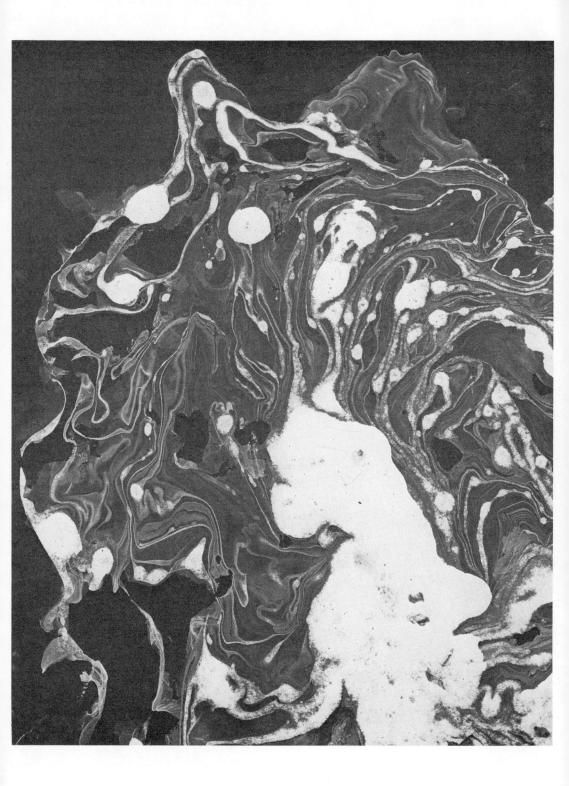

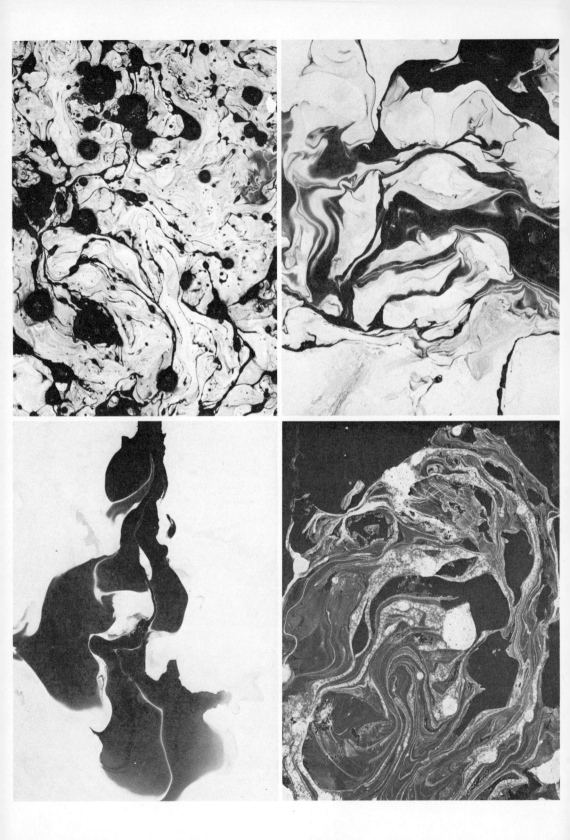

Simple Block Prints

When professional artists make block prints they usually carve their designs in blocks of wood or linoleum. These materials give good results, but the carving can be difficult. The block prints in this chapter are made with materials that are easier to work with. No special carving tools are needed.

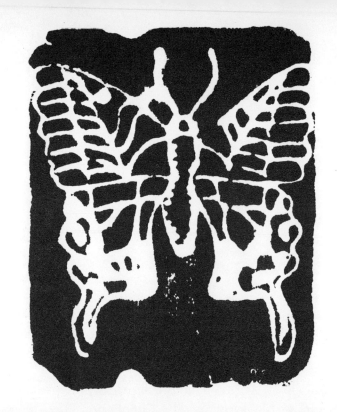

Styrofoam Drawings

Collect a few of the soft styrofoam trays that supermarkets use for holding fruit and vegetables. Cut the sides off the trays, leaving just the flat, smooth bottoms. Use a ball-point pen to draw a different picture or design on each piece of styrofoam. Press just hard enough to make a shallow groove in the styrofoam.

Ink your styrofoam drawings and press them on paper.

Acrylic Blocks

Buy a small jar of acrylic painting medium (available at art supply stores). Brush a thick coat of acrylic medium on a piece of hard cardboard. Wait ten or fifteen minutes, until the

acrylic medium is partially dry. Scratch a design into it, using a toothpick or a pencil point. Wait overnight before printing.

Design left by a paper doily pressed into acrylic, then removed.

Glue Prints

Make a design by dripping rubber cement on a piece of stiff cardboard. Lift the rubber cement out of the bottle with the brush attached to the bottle cap. Let the cement drip from the brush in long lines or loops.

If you have trouble controlling the flow of cement from the brush, try using a drinking straw or a wooden match. If you do not feel comfortable making up a design as you drip the cement, try drawing a picture on the cardboard, then dripping the cement along the lines of your drawing. Let the cement dry overnight before making your first print.

An easier method is to use an ordinary white household glue, such as Elmer's Glue-all. This kind of glue comes in a plastic squeeze bottle with a narrow spout. The narrow spout makes it simple to squeeze out thin lines of glue.

Each method has advantages and disadvantages. White glue is much easier to use, but it sometimes dries unevenly, with unexpected lumps or sunken areas. Rubber cement is more difficult to work with, but it flattens and spreads as it dries, giving prints with a smoother overall texture. Rubber cement printing blocks can also be used to make another kind of print (see p. 89, on resist printing).

Rubber Cement Resist Prints

Buy a sheet of smooth posterboard at an art supply store. Posterboard comes in many different colors. Choose a color that will contrast with the color of the ink that you plan to use. Cut the posterboard into smaller pieces.

Make a rubber cement printing block, following the general instructions on p. 86, but using a piece of posterboard instead of ordinary cardboard.

Do not draw your design on the posterboard. Make up your design as you work, dripping and dabbing the rubber cement on the posterboard.

After the cement dries, ink the printing block and make a few prints. Ink the printing block one more time, but do not

make a print from it. Set it aside to dry. Wait one or two days, to be sure that the ink is very thoroughly dried.

Remove the rubber cement by rubbing it vigorously with your fingertips. The whole piece of posterboard was covered with ink, but the parts protected by a layer of rubber cement will remain the original color.

This resist-printing technique makes use of the special qualities of rubber cement. It will not work with other kinds of glue.

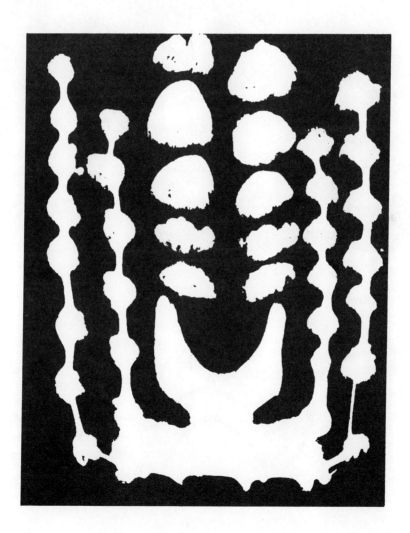

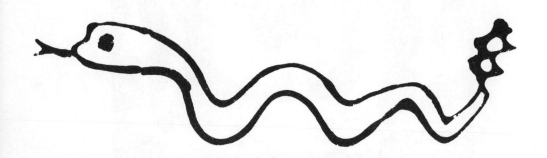

Monotypes

A monotype is a print that can not be repeated—it can be printed only one time.

Buy a small pane of window glass (available at many hardware stores). Smooth the sharp edges of the glass carefully with fine sandpaper.

Spread a medium-thick coat of ink on the glass. Leave an uninked margin around the edges of the glass, so that you can pick it up without putting your fingers in the ink.

Scratch a design into the wet ink with a soft, blunt tool, like a pencil eraser or a lollipop stick. Work as quickly as possible. The design has to be finished before the ink starts to dry.

Cover the inked glass with a sheet of paper. Roll over the paper with a brayer, or rub the paper with your fingers. Lift off the paper. If the ink has squeezed into the lines of your printed design, you may have pressed too hard on the paper, or you may have used too thick a layer of ink. Spread a little more ink over the first design and try again.

Assembled Block Prints

The printing blocks in this chapter are made by gluing various materials to pieces of cardboard. The printing blocks are then brushed with ink and covered with paper. A large, soft brayer is rolled over the paper. If you do not have a brayer, just press the printing block on a sheet of paper. If you have trouble getting a good print, try putting some newspapers or a piece of fabric under the paper, and then pressing the printing block on the paper.

Found Objects
Look for small objects that can be glued flat on a piece of cardboard. All the objects for any one printing block should be of about the same thickness. Otherwise, only the thickest objects will show on the print. Try using toothpicks, bobby pins, flat metal washers, old keys, broken matchsticks, or any other objects you can find. Arrange the objects in a pattern on a piece of cardboard. Glue them to the cardboard. Wait for the glue to dry before printing.

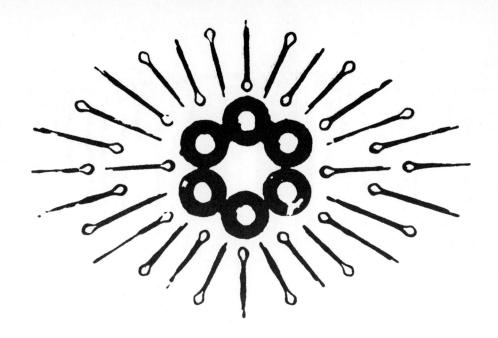

ABOVE: *Cotter pins and metal washers*

BELOW: *Paper clips and flip top rings*

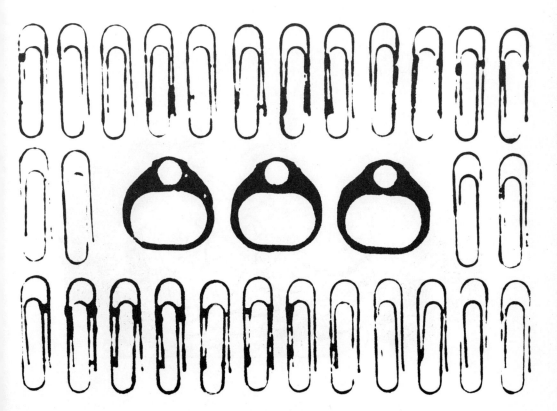

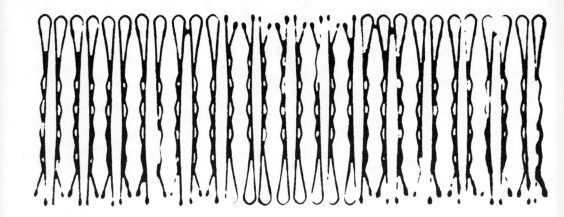

Bobby pins

String Prints

Pull some thread from a spool. Form it into a loosely tangled ball. Spread glue on a piece of cardboard. Flatten the ball of thread into the glue. Wet your fingers and pat the thread down flat on the cardboard.

Cut some random lengths of string. Squeeze out some glue on a piece of thick cardboard. Use the edge of an index card or a matchbook to spread the glue evenly on the cardboard. Press pieces of string into the glue. Pat the string down with your fingers to make sure it will stick.

Make loops of thread by winding it several times around your fingers or around a loosely crumpled paper napkin. Build up a design by pressing loops of thread on glued cardboard. Wetting the loops will help the thread to absorb more of the glue and stick more tightly to the cardboard.

Noodle Prints
Make a design by gluing broken pieces of uncooked spaghetti to a piece of cardboard.

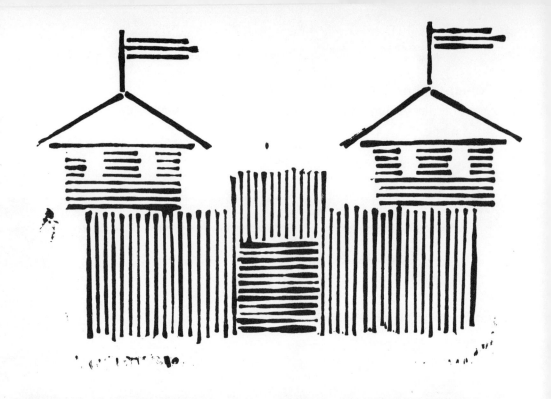

Try using elbow macaroni.

Try printing with alphabet noodles. Glue the letters and numbers to a strip of cardboard. Try to use noodles that are all the same thickness. The left side of your print will be made from the right side of the cardboard strip, so glue the noodles on backwards, reading from right to left.

Wait for the glue to dry. Make a sample print. If some noodles are thicker than others, the thinner ones will not print clearly. Rub the noodles lightly with a fine sandpaper, until all the noodles are the same thickness.

MERRY CHRISTMAS

SEASONS GREETINGS

HAPPY BIRTHDAY

CHARLES BURKE
3257 HILLTOP DRIVE

Paper and Fabric Collages
Find some scraps of textured fabric or paper—lace, burlap, disposable dishcloths, paper doilies, or any other thin material with an interesting surface pattern. Try using bits of string, crumpled aluminum foil, or sections cut from mesh produce bags.

Arrange some scraps to form a design on a piece of thick cardboard. Use scraps the way you find them, or cut or rip them to get whatever shapes you want. Pay no attention to the colors of the scraps, only the surface textures. They will all be printed in the same color.

106

When you feel satisfied with your design, glue the scraps to the cardboard. Wait for the glue to dry. Brush on a heavy coat of ink. Wait for this first coat of ink to dry. The dried ink will stiffen the textures of the various materials, and keep them from getting soggy when you make several prints from the same block.

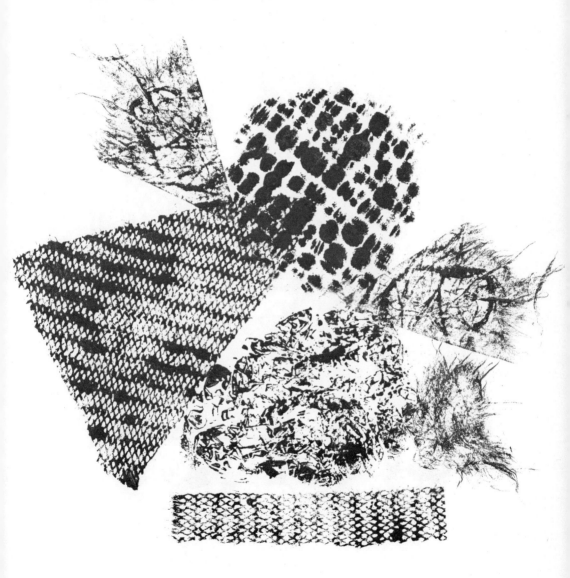

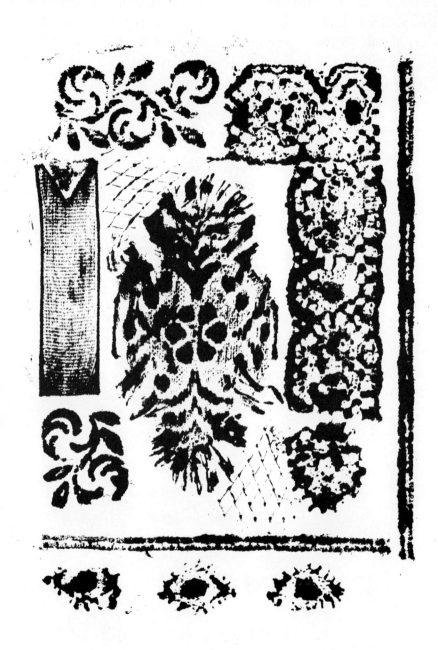

Cardboard Cutout Block Prints

Find a piece of cardboard thin enough to be cut easily with scissors. Try using an empty cereal box, or some other empty food container.

Cut some thin cardboard into small pieces. Build up a design by gluing some of these pieces to a printing block of thick cardboard. Wait for the glue to dry completely before printing.

A thin cardboard silhouette, cut with sharp manicure scissors.

A 4-inch square of cardboard, cut into strips. The strips were separated slightly when they were glued to the block.

Printing
on
Fabric

Make a few prints on scraps of cloth, instead of on sheets of paper. The texture of the cloth will add a new element to the design. Smooth, finely woven fabrics are the easiest to print on. Thick, woolly, or strongly textured fabrics are more difficult to work with. Not all printmaking methods will work well on fabric. Try using found objects, a clay printing stamp, a few large eraser stamps, or a stencil.

If you enjoy sewing, you may want to make curtains, bed-spreads, or clothing, using fabric decorated with your own printed designs.

Regular water soluble printing ink should not be used on any fabric that might have to be washed. Art supply stores sell special inks for printing on fabric. You will also need a special solvent, such as turpentine, for thinning the ink and cleaning your hands and tools. Ask the sales clerk to recommend a solvent that can be used for thinning the particular brand of ink that you buy.

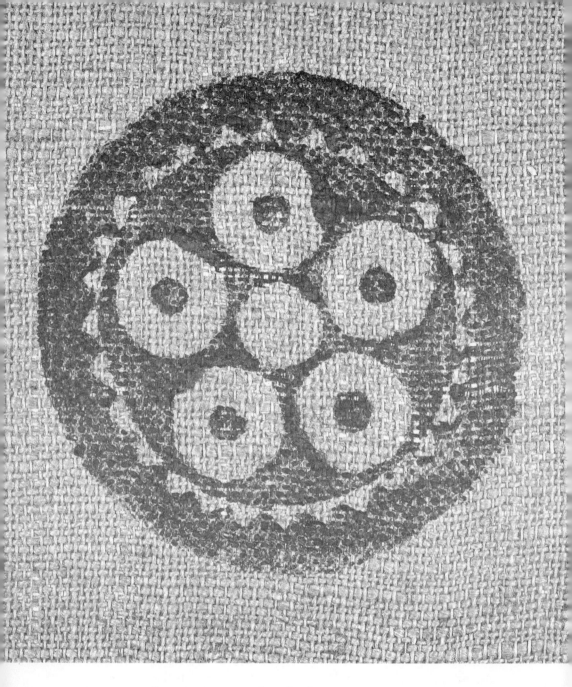

ABOVE: *A clay stamp, printed on burlap.*

OPPOSITE: *African fabric patterns made with handcarved printing stamps. From Williams:* AFRICAN DESIGNS, *Dover Publications, Inc.*

Printing a large piece of fabric is a lot of work. Start with a relatively small fabric printing project, like making a printed wall hanging or printing decorative borders across the ends of a pillowcase.

Always buy a piece of fabric slightly longer than the length you will need to make your project. Use the extra material for making sample prints, to figure out exactly how much ink to use and how hard to press when you make each print.

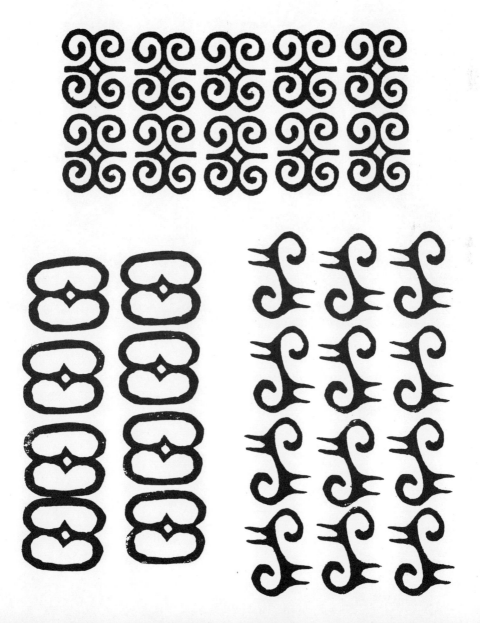

ABOVE AND OPPOSITE: *Delicate Japanese stencil patterns, used for printing colorful designs on fabric. From Tuer:* JAPANESE STENCIL DESIGNS, *Dover Publications, Inc.*

Further Reading

If you want to learn more about printmaking, check in your local library or bookstore for some of the following books:

Brommer, Gerald F. *Relief Printmaking*. Worcester, Mass., Davis Publications, Inc., 1970.
  A good introduction to linoleum block printing and woodcut block printing, with short chapters on simpler printmaking methods.

Capon, Robin. *Introducing Abstract Printmaking*. New York, Watson-Guptill Publications, 1973.
  Simple block prints and linoleum block prints. Tips on printmaking using two or three colors, or combining several printmaking methods to produce more interesting prints.

Erickson, Janet. *Block Printing on Textiles*. New York, Watson-Guptill Publications, 1961, reprinted 1974.
  Clear directions for simple and complex fabric printing

methods. Useful information on the special qualities of different fabrics—textures, shrinkage rates, best printing techniques for each type of fabric, etc.

Green, Peter. *New Creative Print Making*. New York, Watson-Guptill Publications, 1965.
An excellent, easy-to-read book on simple printmaking methods, with many fine illustrations.

Laliberte, Norman & Mogelon, Alex. *The Art of Monoprint*. New York, Van Nostrand Reinhold, 1974.
An excellent book on monotype printmaking techniques, using simple, inexpensive materials. Many beautiful illustrations.

Russ, Stephen. *Fabric Printing by Hand*. New York, Watson-Guptill Publications, 1965.
A useful book for the beginner or the professional artist. Easy fabric printing processes—tie-dye, batik, block printing, silk screening, etc.

Schachner, Erwin. *Step by Step Printmaking*. Racine, Wisconsin, Western Publishing Company, Inc. (Golden Press), 1970.
A good guidebook for making prints combining several colors, using hand printing methods or a small home printing press. Not for beginners. Available in paperback in many bookstores.

Wenniger, Mary A. *Collagraph Printmaking*. New York, Watson-Guptill Publications, 1975.
A complete survey of printmaking from collage-type printing blocks, using found materials, fabric, string, paper, etc.

Index

ABOUT THE AUTHOR

Peter Weiss is the author of *Balsa Wood Craft* and co-author, with Carol Weiss, of *Cutting Up With Paper*. Mr. Weiss has a variety of hobbies, including painting, wood sculpture, and building his own furniture. He also enjoys traveling and has camped in many areas of the United States, as well as in Canada. Mr. Weiss is a college bookstore manager.